Matchstick

MA TH

puzzles

This
Book
belongs
to

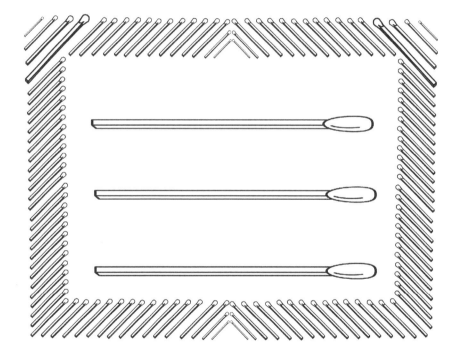

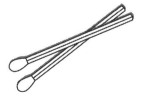

GAME RULES

1. Read the content of the task.

  EXAMPLE: Add only one matchstick to make a correct equation.

2. Look at the picture.
  EXAMPLE:

3. Use all moves and correct the equation.
  EXAMPLE:

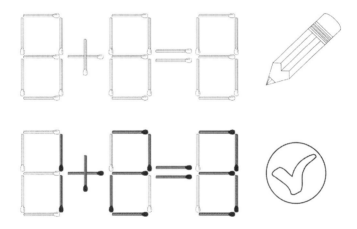

4. Check the correct solution on the last pages of the book.

5. If you have made all the moves and the equation is correct and the answer is different from the one in the last pages of the book, then you are a master.

6. Have fun and good luck solving the tasks.

SCRATCHPAD

1. Add only 1 matchstick to make a correct equation.

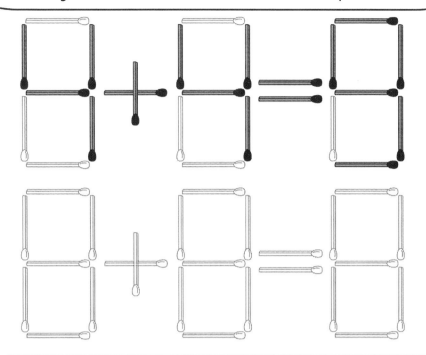

2. Move only 4 matchsticks to make a correct equation.

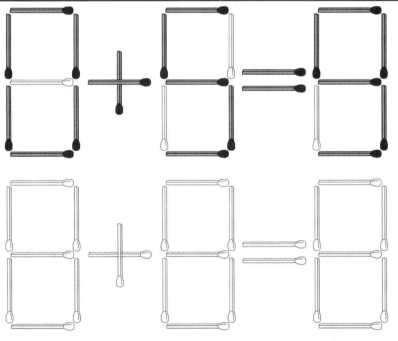

The solution is on page 115.

SCRATCHPAD

3. Add only 1 matchstick to make a correct equation.

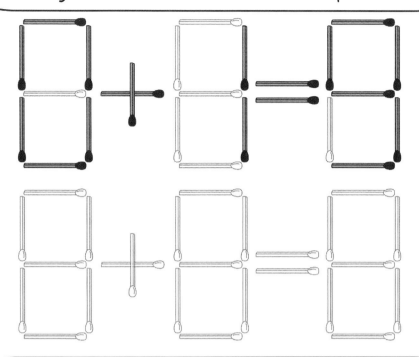

4. Add only 6 matchsticks to make a correct equation.

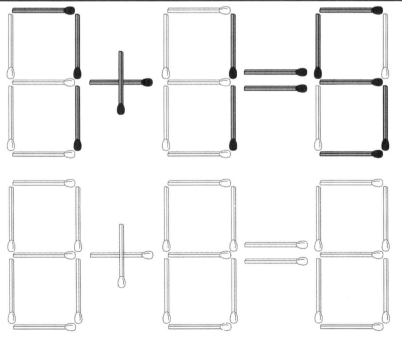

The solution is on page 115.

SCRATCHPAD

5. Remove only 1 matchstick to make a correct equation.

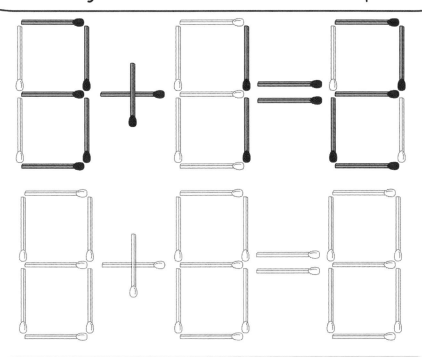

6. Remove only 3 matchsticks to make a correct equation.

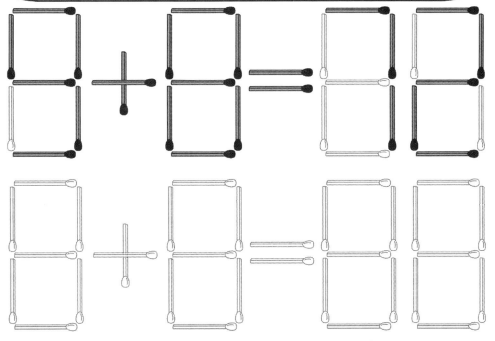

The solution is on page 116.

11

SCRATCHPAD

7. Add only 1 matchstick to make a correct equation.

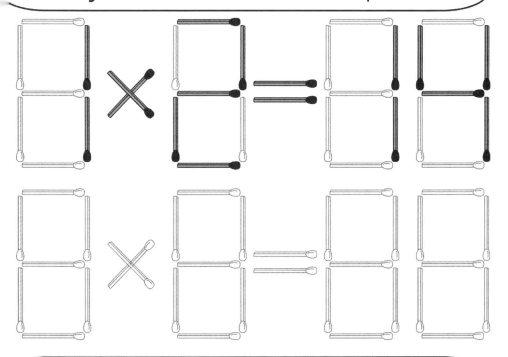

8. Add only 4 matchsticks to make a correct equation.

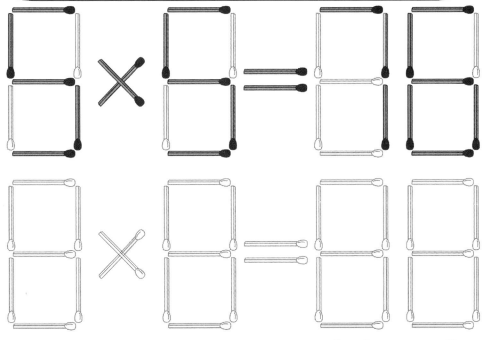

The solution is on page 116.

SCRATCHPAD

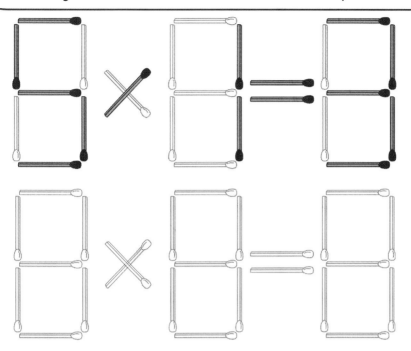

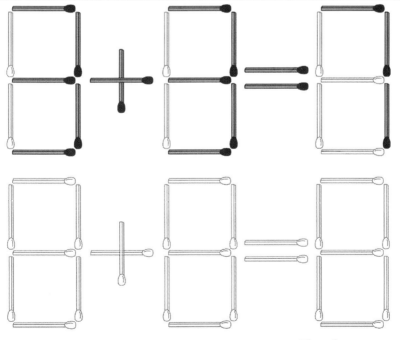

The solution is on page 117.

SCRATCHPAD

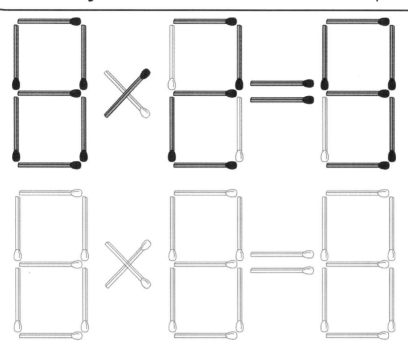

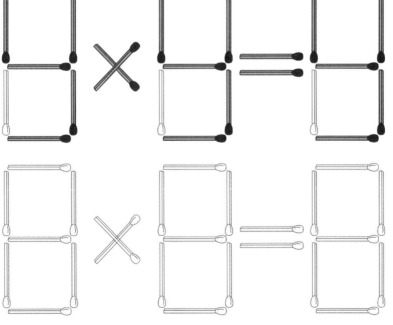

The solution is on page 117.

17

SCRATCHPAD

13. Move only 1 matchstick to make a correct equation.

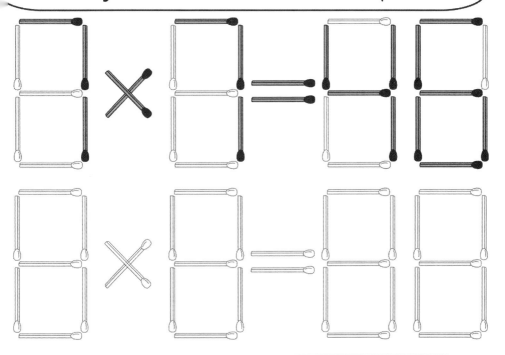

14. Move only 3 matchsticks to make a correct equation.

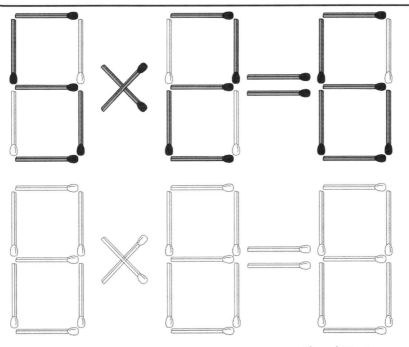

The solution is on page 118.

SCRATCHPAD

15. Add only 1 matchstick to make a correct equation.

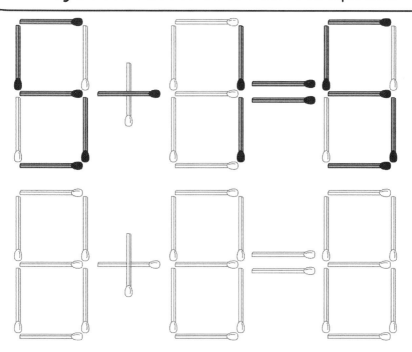

16. Remove only 3 matchsticks to make a correct equation.

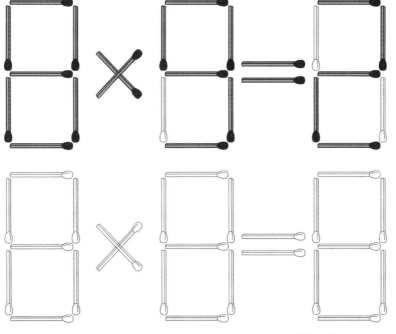

The solution is on page 118.

SCRATCHPAD

17. Remove only 1 matchstick to make a correct equation.

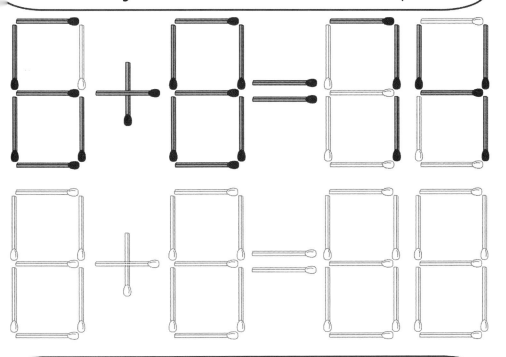

18. Add only 2 matchsticks to make a correct equation.

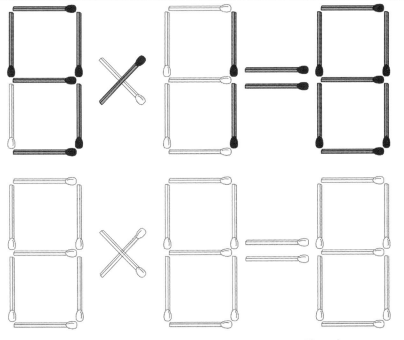

The solution is on page 119.

23

SCRATCHPAD

19. Remove only 2 matchsticks to make a correct equation.

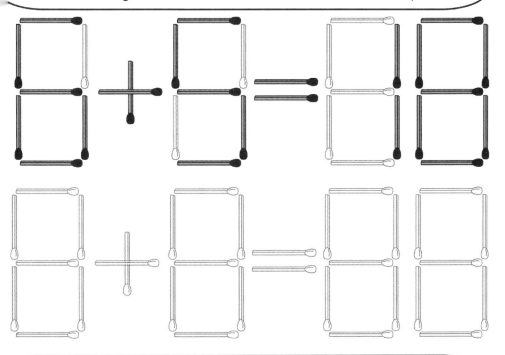

20. Move only 2 matchsticks to make a correct equation.

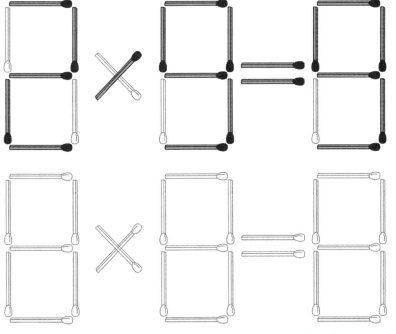

The solution is on page 119.

SCRATCHPAD

21. Add only 1 matchstick to make a correct equation.

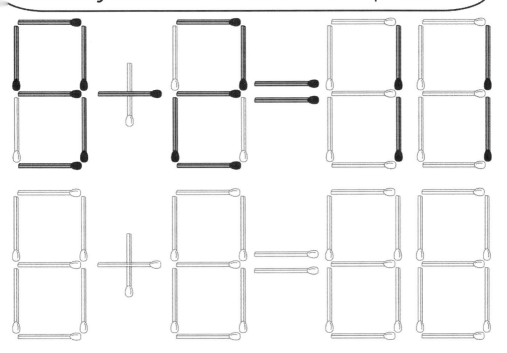

22. Remove only 3 matchsticks to make a correct equation.

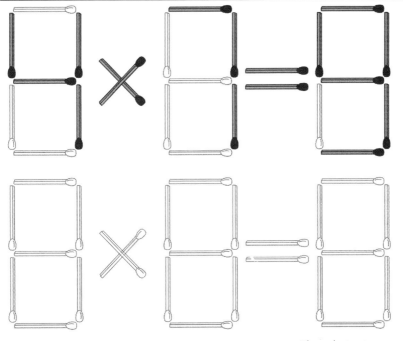

The solution is on page 120.

SCRATCHPAD

23. Move only 1 matchstick to make a correct equation.

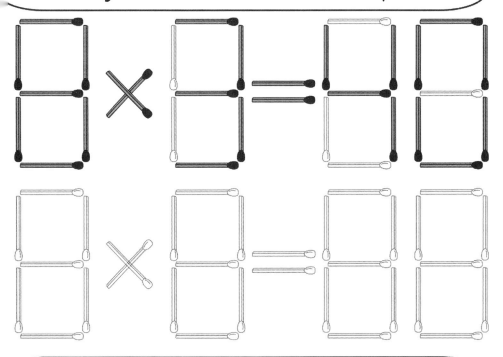

24. Move only 3 matchsticks to make a correct equation.

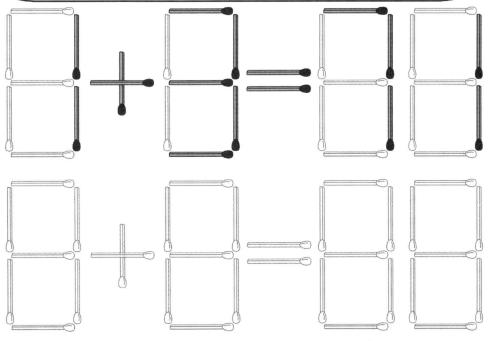

The solution is on page 120.

SCRATCHPAD

25. Add only 1 matchstick to make a correct equation.

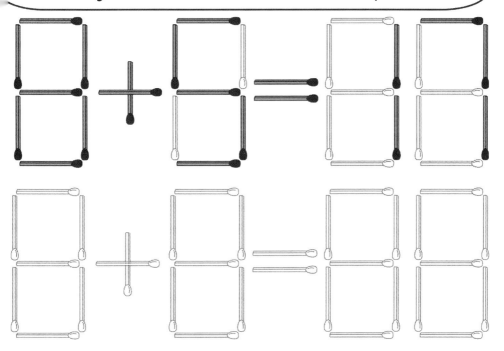

26. Move only 2 matchsticks to make a correct equation.

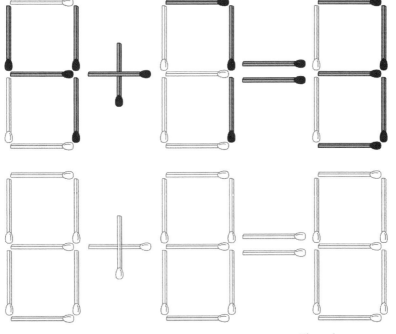

The solution is on page 121.

SCRATCHPAD

27. Move only 1 matchstick to make a correct equation.

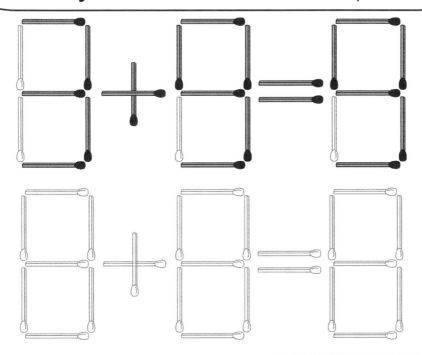

28. Remove only 4 matchsticks to make a correct equation.

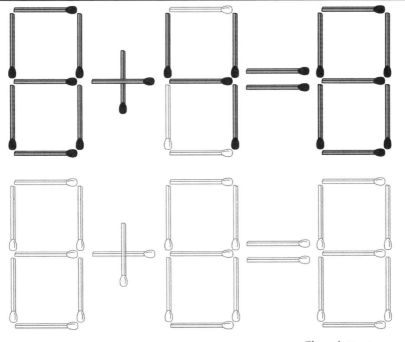

The solution is on page 121.

33

SCRATCHPAD

29. Remove only 1 matchstick to make a correct equation.

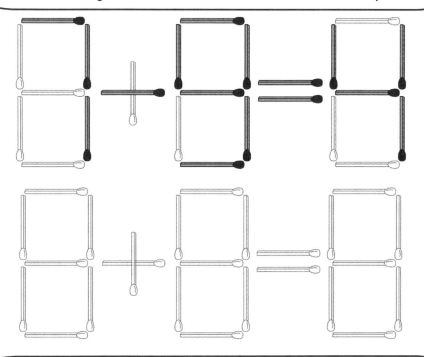

30. Move only 2 matchsticks to make a correct equation.

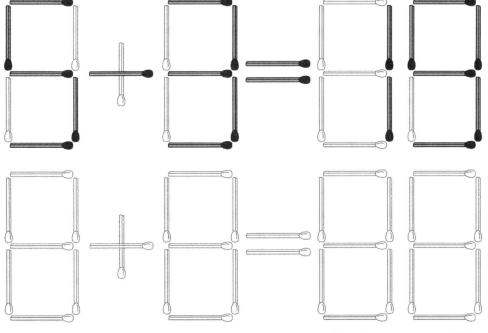

The solution is on page 122.

SCRATCHPAD

31. Add only 1 matchstick to make a correct equation.

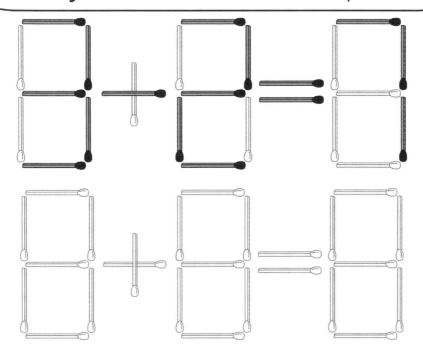

32. Add only 1 matchstick to make a correct equation.

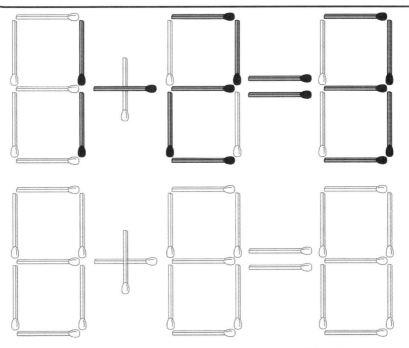

The solution is on page 122.

SCRATCHPAD

33. Add only 1 matchstick to make a correct equation.

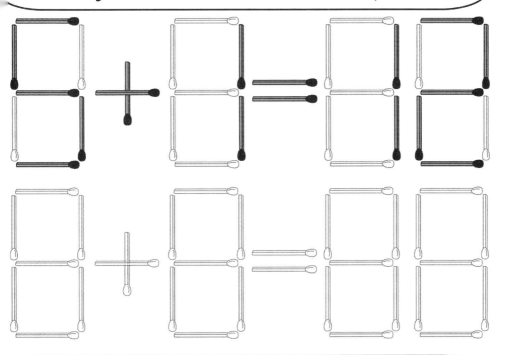

34. Move only 3 matchsticks to make a correct equation.

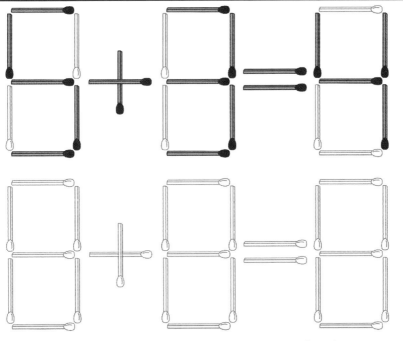

The solution is on page 123.

SCRATCHPAD

35. Move only 2 matchsticks to make a correct equation.

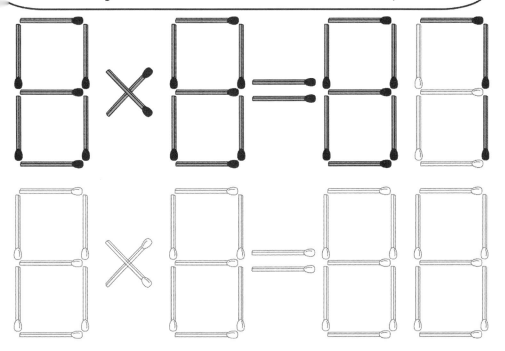

36. Remove only 2 matchsticks to make a correct equation.

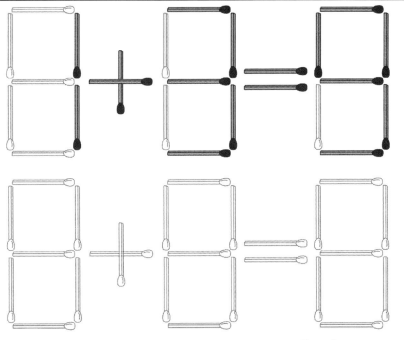

The solution is on page 123.

SCRATCHPAD

37. Move only 2 matchsticks to make a correct equation.

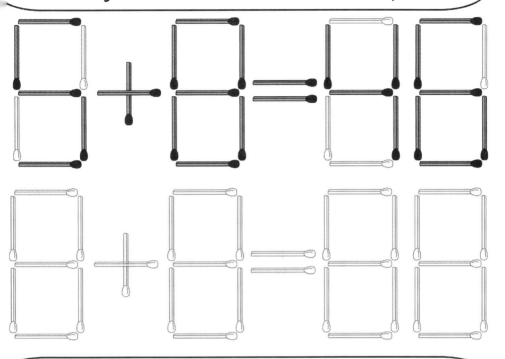

38. Add only 1 matchstick to make a correct equation.

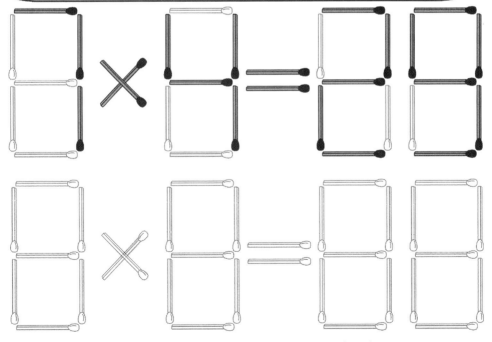

The solution is on page 124.

SCRATCHPAD

39. Move only 2 matchsticks to make a correct equation.

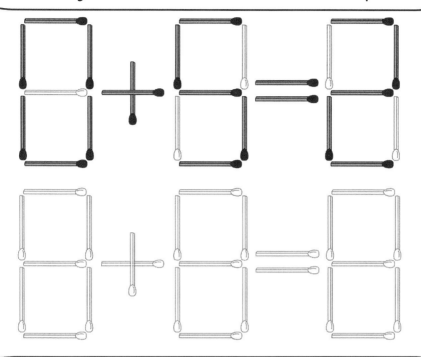

40. Move only 2 matchsticks to make a correct equation.

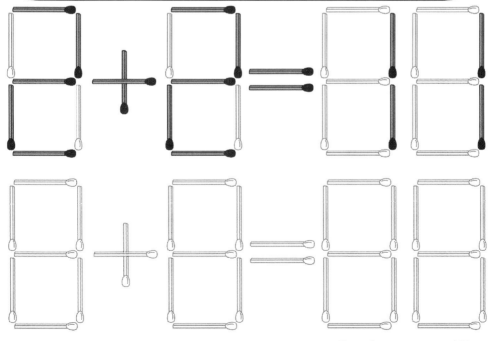

The solution is on page 124.

SCRATCHPAD

41. Move only 1 matchstick to make a correct equation.

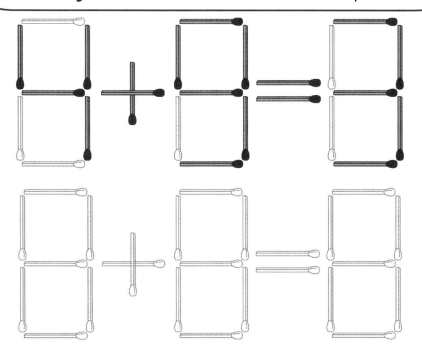

42. Move only 2 matchsticks to make a correct equation.

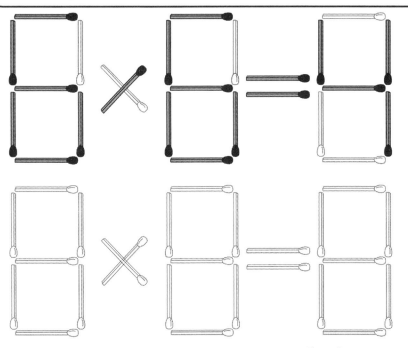

The solution is on page 125.

SCRATCHPAD

43. Add only 1 matchstick to make a correct equation.

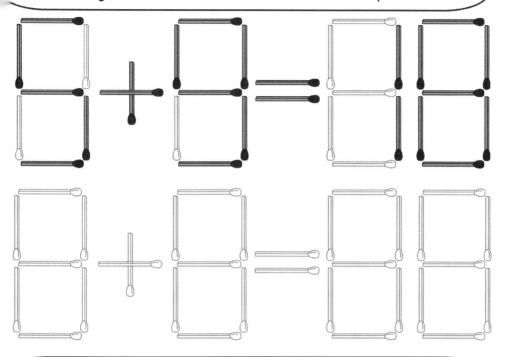

44. Add only 1 matchstick to make a correct equation.

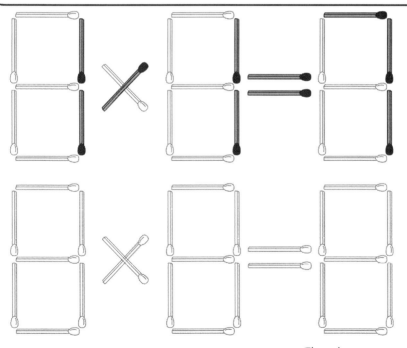

The solution is on page 125.

SCRATCHPAD

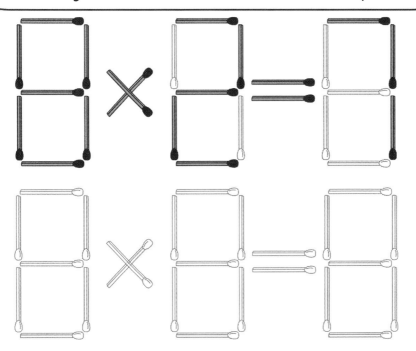

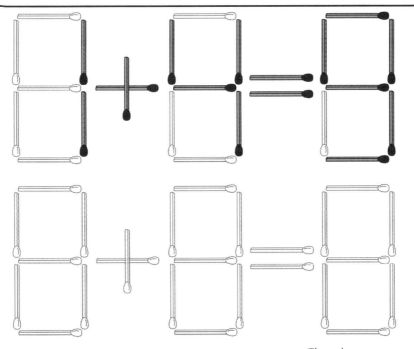

The solution is on page 126.

51

SCRATCHPAD

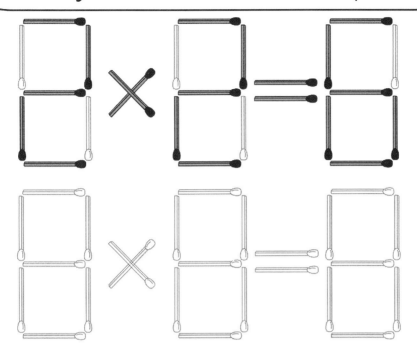

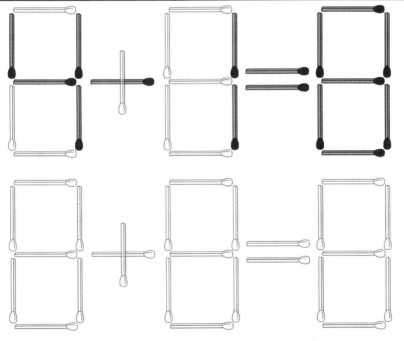

The solution is on page 126.

53

SCRATCHPAD

49. Move only 2 matchsticks to make a correct equation.

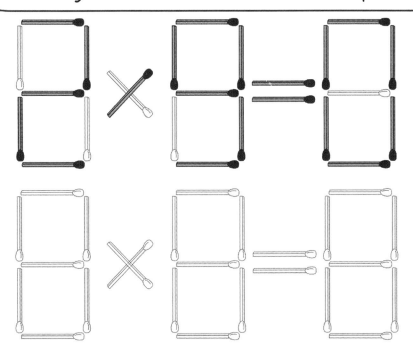

50. Remove only 1 matchstick to make a correct equation.

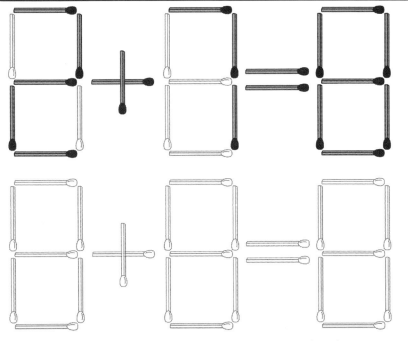

The solution is on page 127.

SCRATCHPAD

51. Remove only 2 matchsticks to make a correct equation.

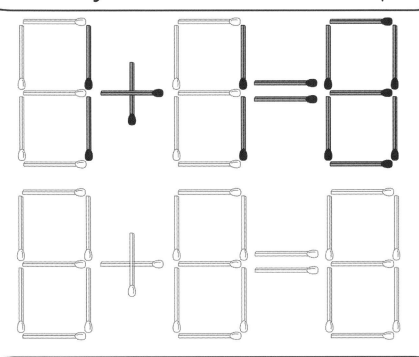

52. Remove only 1 matchstick to make a correct equation.

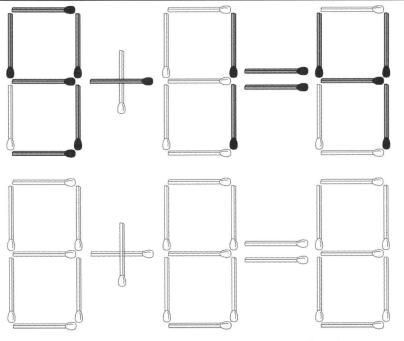

The solution is on page 127.

SCRATCHPAD

53. Move only 1 matchstick to make a correct equation.

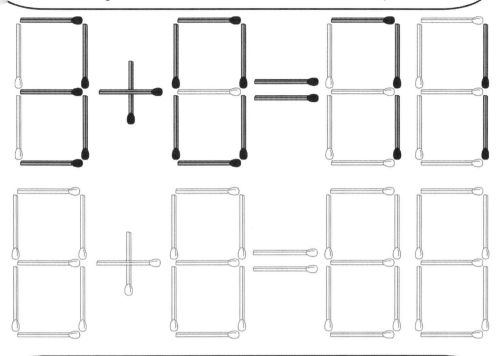

54. Remove only 1 matchstick to make a correct equation.

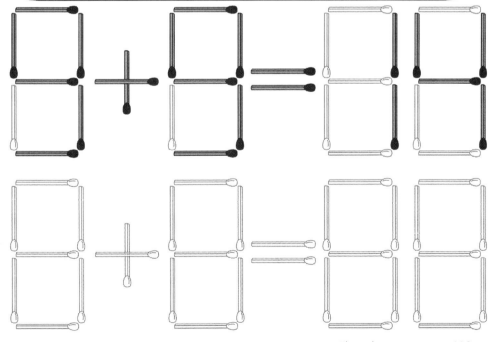

The solution is on page 128.

SCRATCHPAD

55. Add only 1 matchstick to make a correct equation.

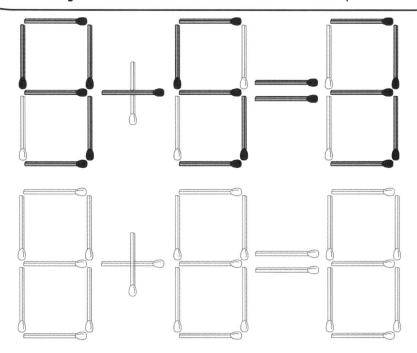

56. Remove only 1 matchstick to make a correct equation.

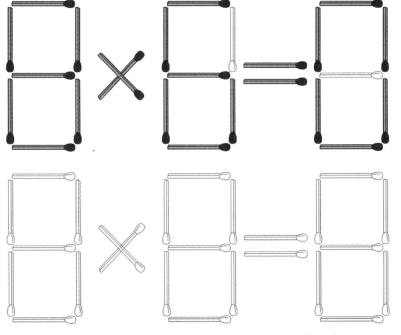

The solution is on page 128.

SCRATCHPAD

57. Move only 3 matchsticks to make a correct equation.

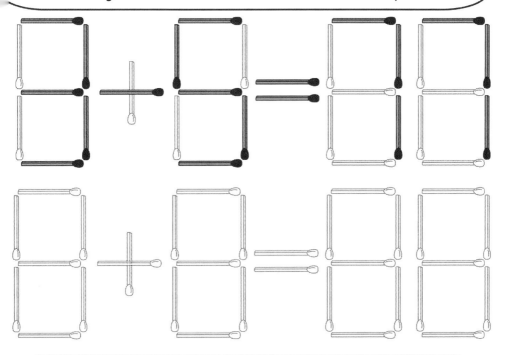

58. Move only 1 matchstick to make a correct equation.

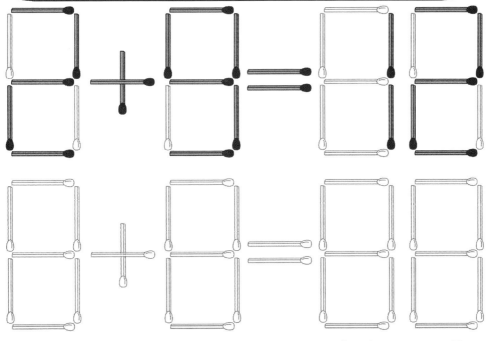

The solution is on page 129.

SCRATCHPAD

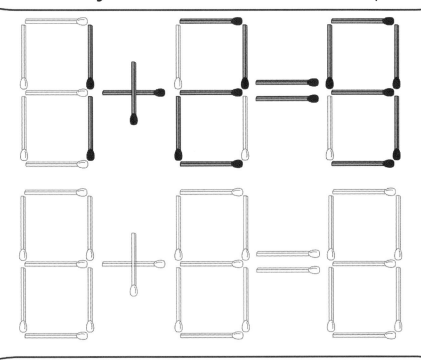

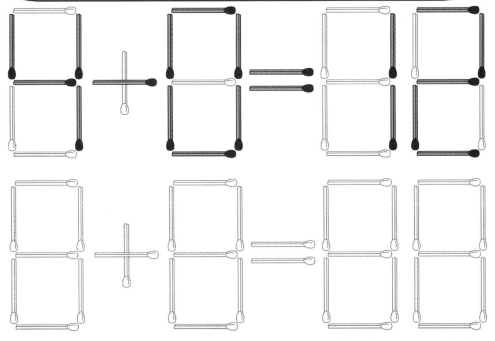

The solution is on page 129.

SCRATCHPAD

61. Move only 3 matchsticks to make a correct equation.

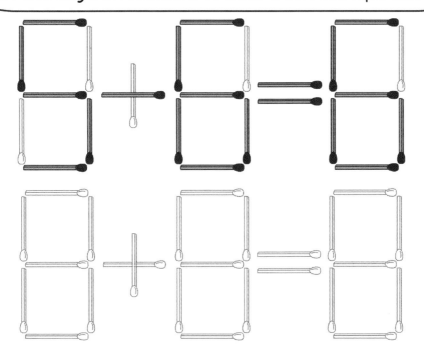

62. Add only 2 matchsticks to make a correct equation.

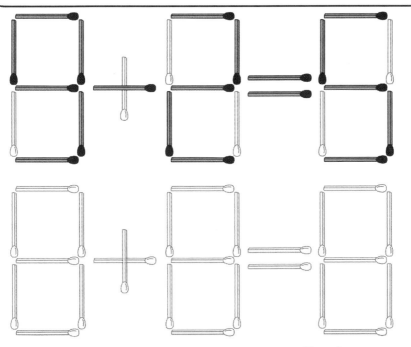

The solution is on page 130.

SCRATCHPAD

63. Add only 2 matchsticks to make a correct equation.

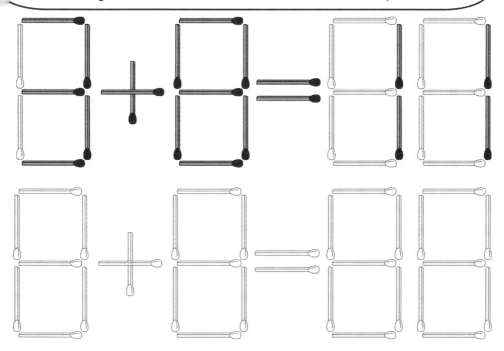

64. Add only 3 matchsticks to make a correct equation.

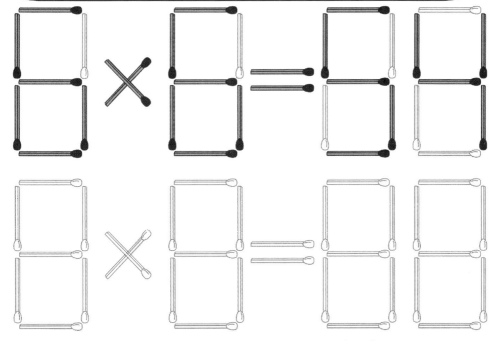

The solution is on page 130.

SCRATCHPAD

65. Move only 1 matchstick to make a correct equation.

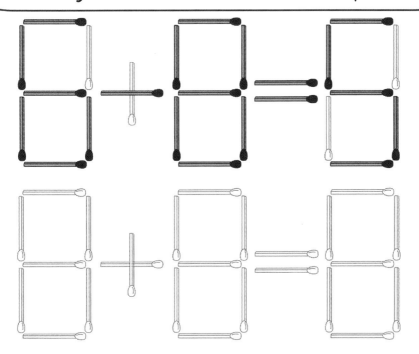

66. Remove only 1 matchstick to make a correct equation.

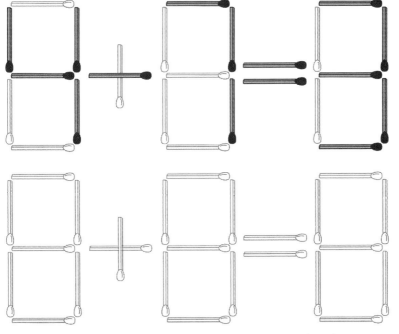

The solution is on page 131.

71

SCRATCHPAD

67. Remove only 1 matchstick to make a correct equation.

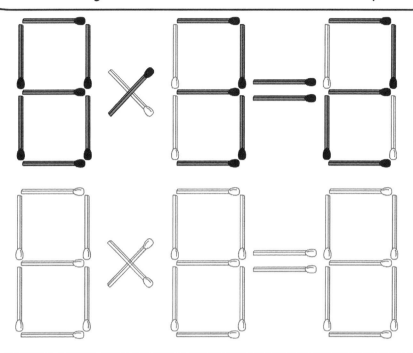

68. Remove only 1 matchstick to make a correct equation.

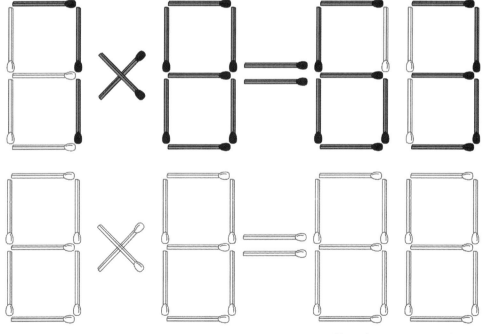

The solution is on page 131.

SCRATCHPAD

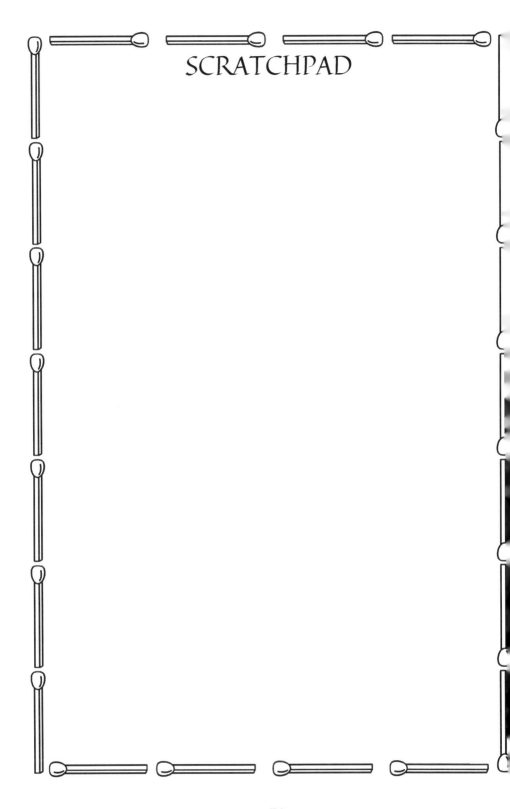

69. Move only 1 matchstick to make a correct equation.

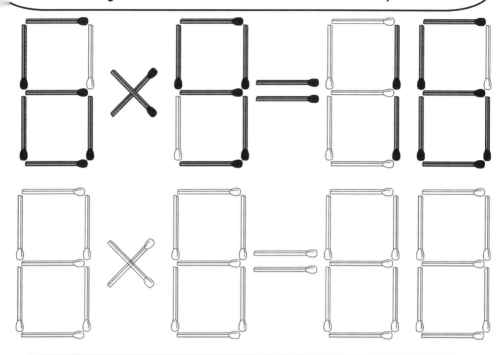

70. Add only 1 matchstick to make a correct equation.

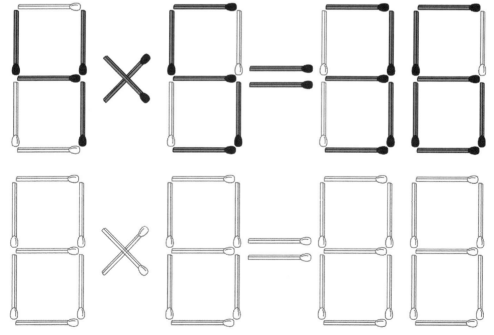

The solution is on page 132.

SCRATCHPAD

71. Add only 2 matchsticks to make a correct equation.

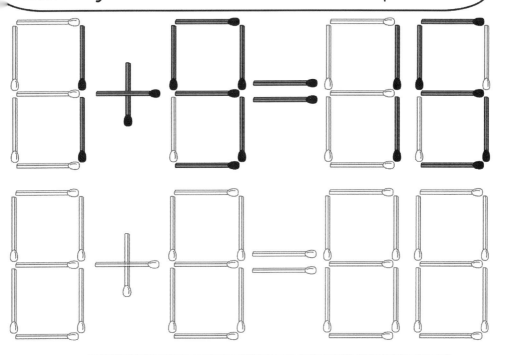

72. Move only 2 matchsticks to make a correct equation.

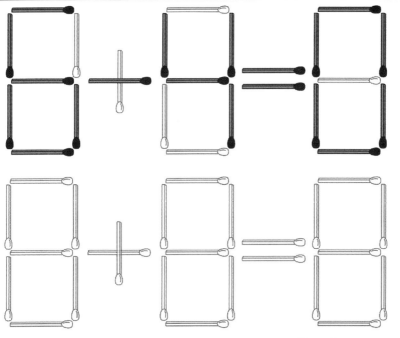

The solution is on page 132.

SCRATCHPAD

73. Add only 2 matchsticks to make a correct equation.

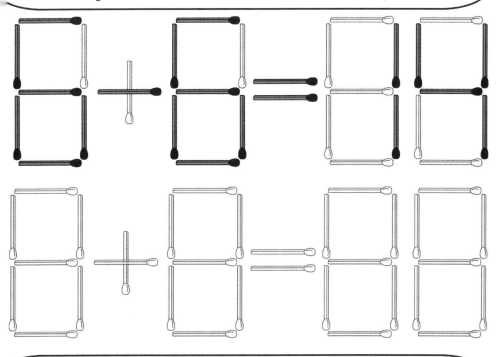

74. Move only 2 matchsticks to make a correct equation.

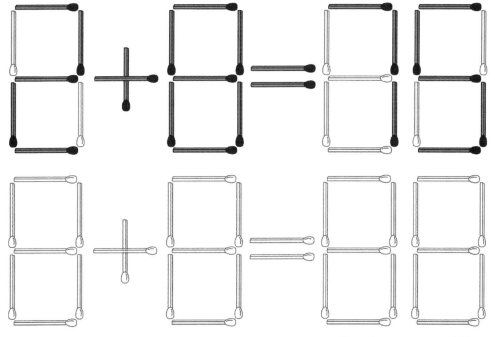

The solution is on page 133.

SCRATCHPAD

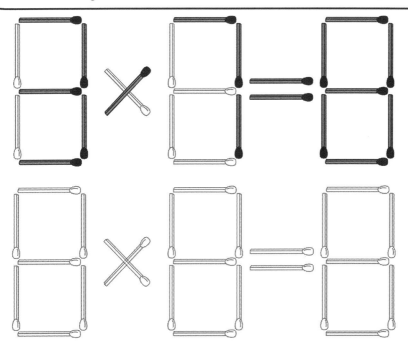

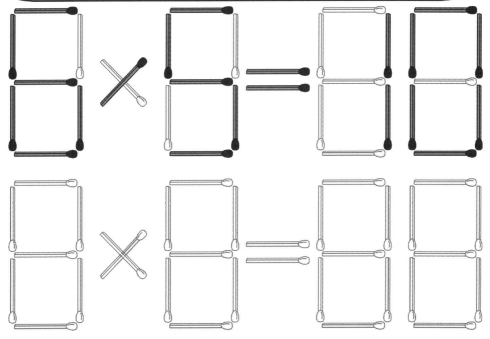

The solution is on page 133.

81

SCRATCHPAD

77. Remove only 2 matchsticks to make a correct equation.

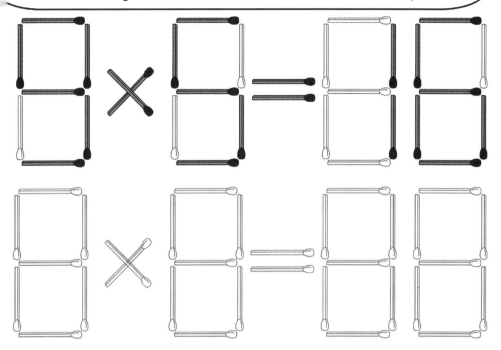

78. Move only 5 matchsticks to make a correct equation.

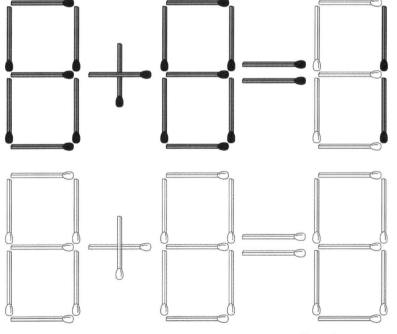

The solution is on page 134.

SCRATCHPAD

79. Move only 2 matchsticks to make a correct equation.

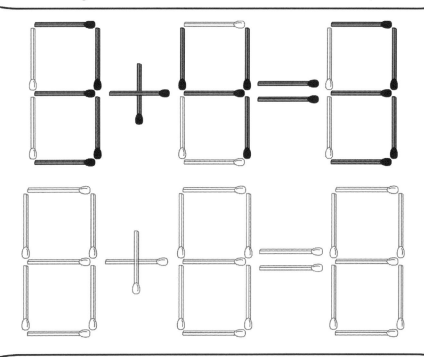

80. Move only 4 matchsticks to make a correct equation.

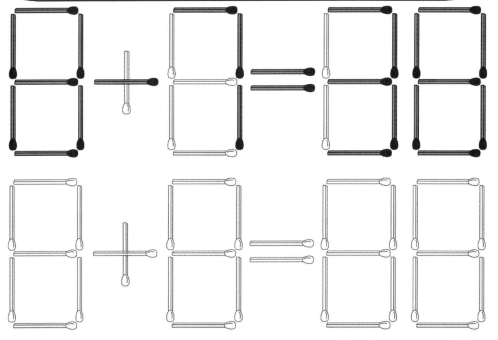

SCRATCHPAD

81. Move only 5 matchsticks to make a correct equation.

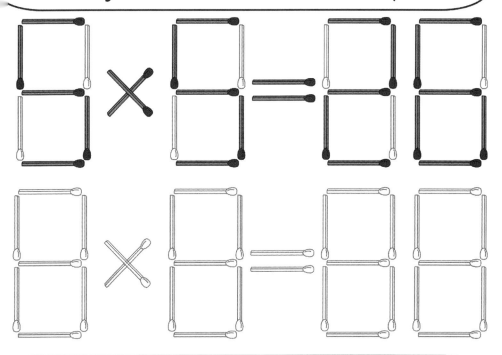

82. Move only 2 matchsticks to make a correct equation.

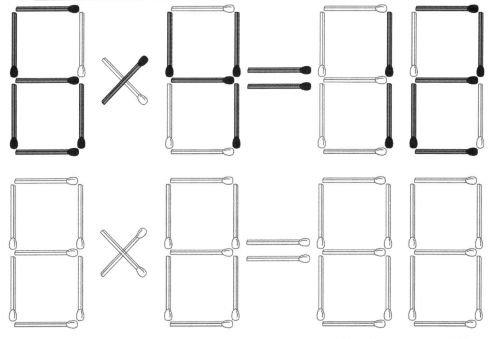

The solution is on page 135.

SCRATCHPAD

83. Move only 2 matchsticks to make a correct equation.

84. Remove only 2 matchsticks to make a correct equation.

The solution is on page 135.

SCRATCHPAD

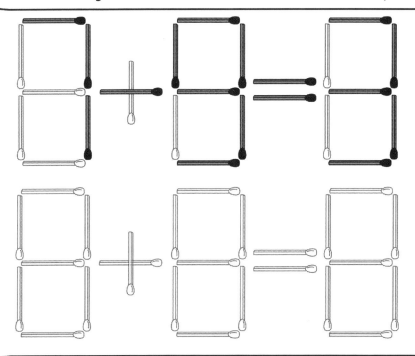

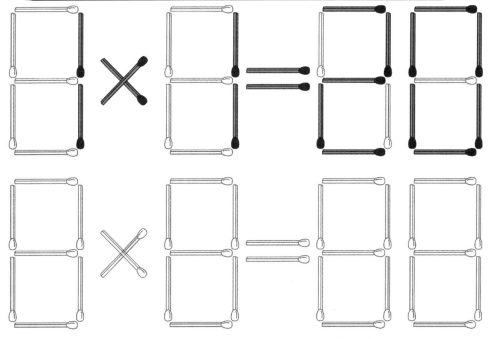

The solution is on page 136.

SCRATCHPAD

87. Move only 2 matchsticks to make a correct equation.

$$8 \times 8 = 88$$

88. Remove only 1 matchstick to make a correct equation.

$$9 + 8 = 88$$

The solution is on page 136.

SCRATCHPAD

89. Add only 4 matchsticks to make a correct equation.

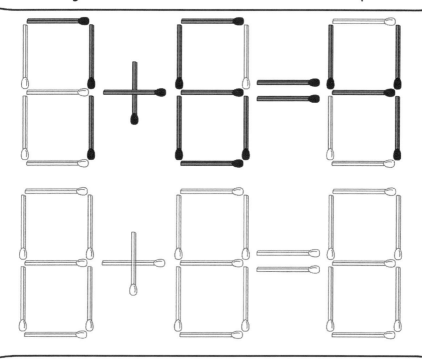

90. Remove only 3 matchsticks to make a correct equation.

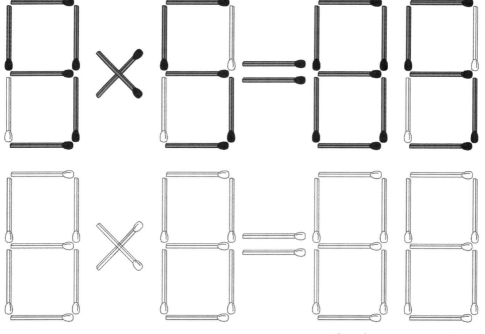

The solution is on page 137.

SCRATCHPAD

91. Remove only 4 matchsticks to make a correct equation.

92. Move only 3 matchsticks to make a correct equation.

The solution is on page 137.

SCRATCHPAD

93. Move only 1 matchstick to make a correct equation.

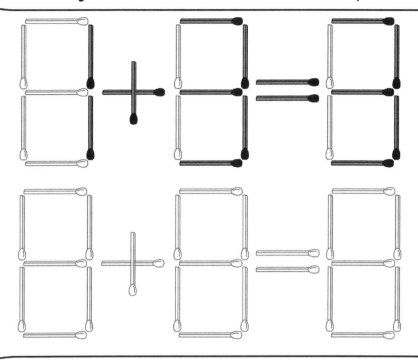

94. Move only 3 matchsticks to make a correct equation.

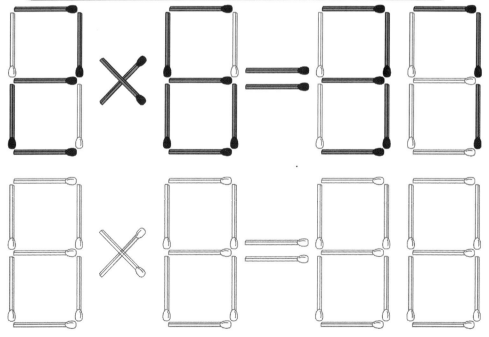

The solution is on page 138.

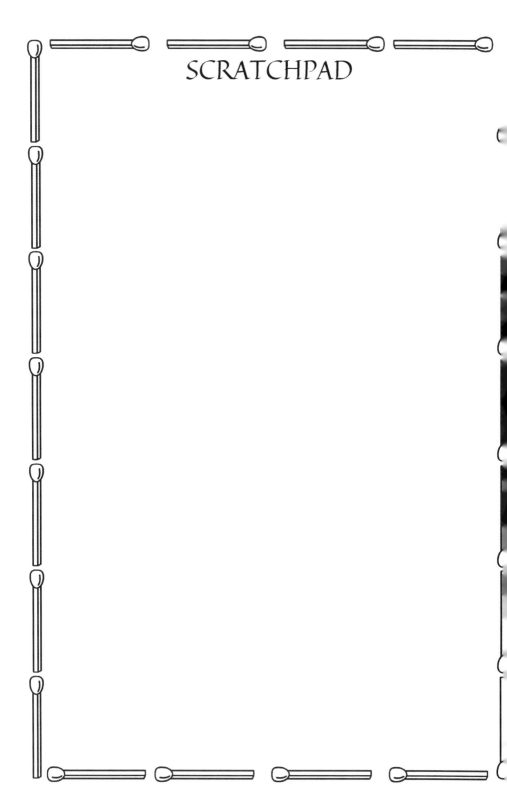

SCRATCHPAD

95. Add only 2 matchsticks to make a correct equation.

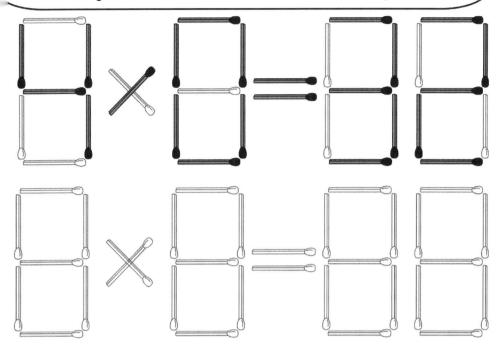

96. Remove only 3 matchsticks to make a correct equation.

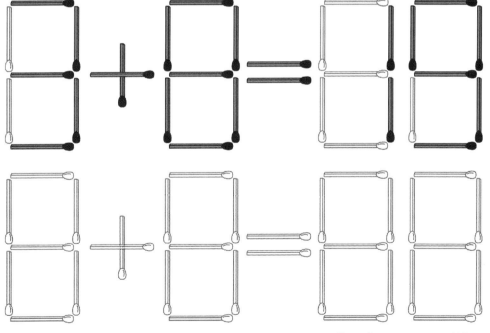

The solution is on page 138.

SCRATCHPAD

97. Remove only 2 matchsticks to make a correct equation.

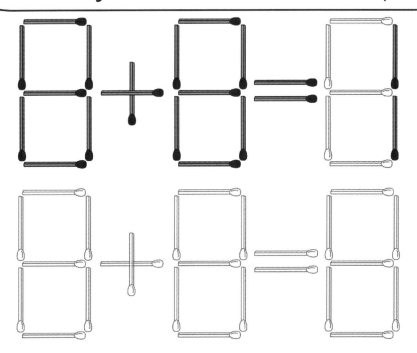

98. Add only 4 matchsticks to make a correct equation.

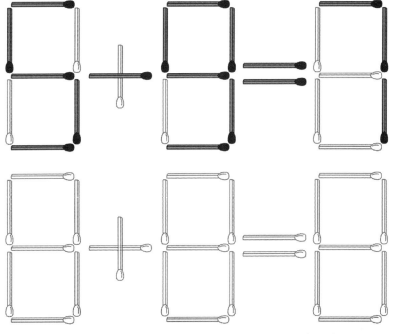

The solution is on page 139.

SCRATCHPAD

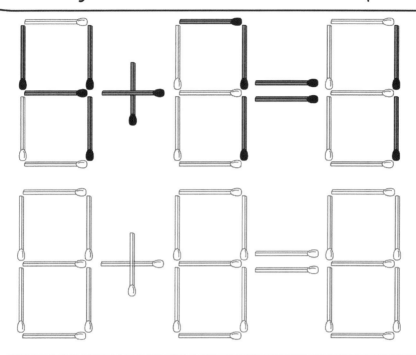

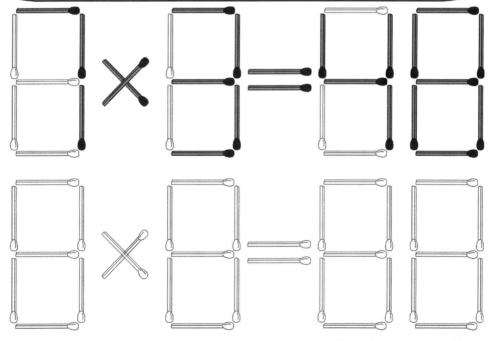

The solution is on page 139.

SCRATCHPAD

BONUS

1. Add only 2 matchsticks to get 4 squares.

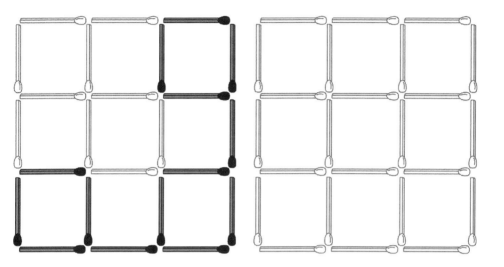

2. Move only 3 matchsticks to get 3 squares.

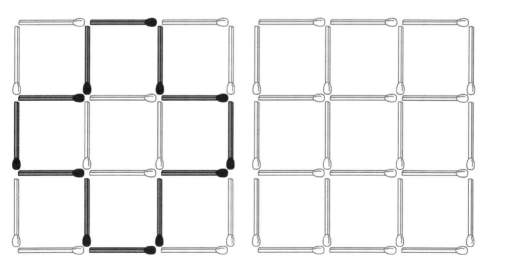

The solution is on page 140.

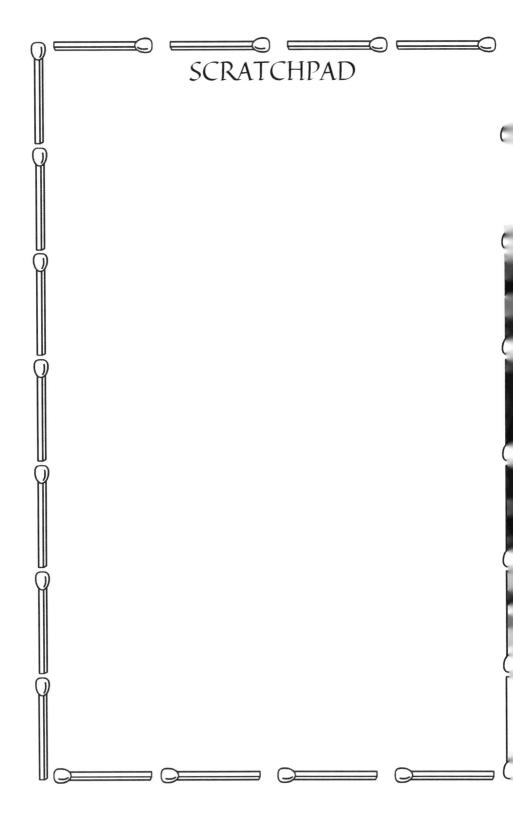

SCRATCHPAD

BONUS

3. Add only 4 matchsticks to get 4 squares.

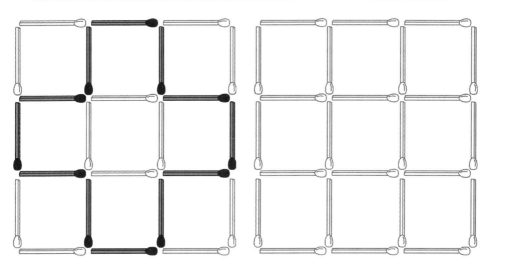

4. Remove only 2 matchsticks to get 3 squares.

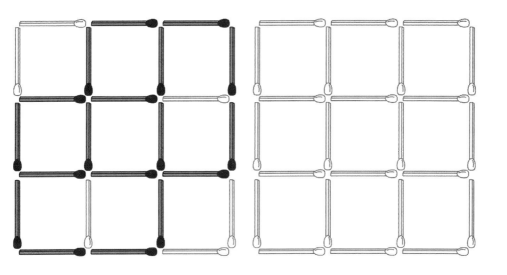

The solution is on page 140.

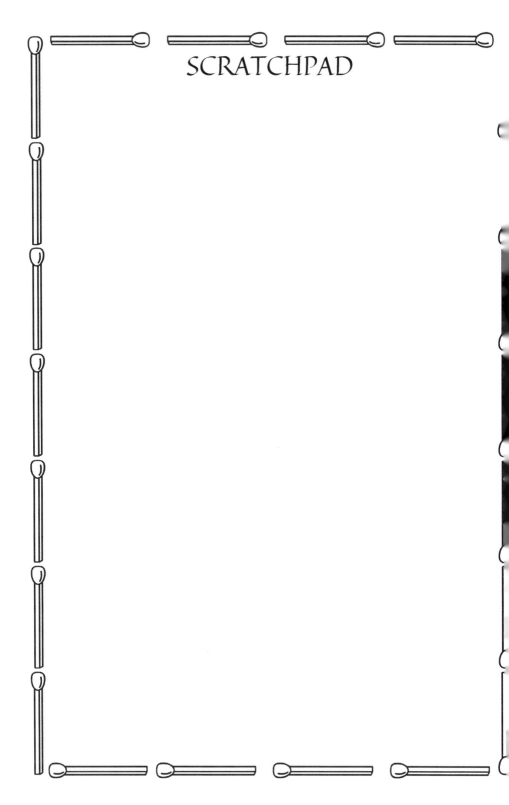

SCRATCHPAD

BONUS

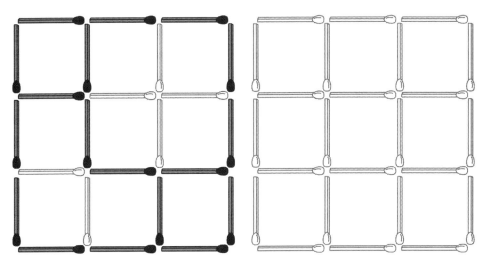

6. Move only 2 matchsticks to get 2 squares.

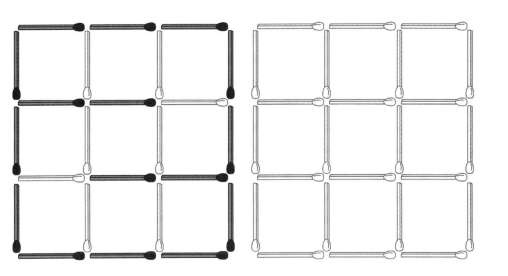

The solution is on page 141.

111

SCRATCHPAD

BONUS

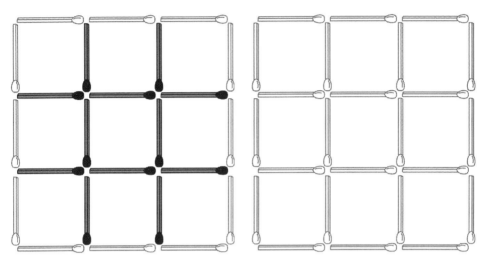

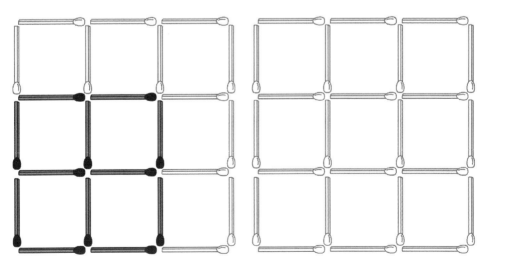

The solution is on page 141.

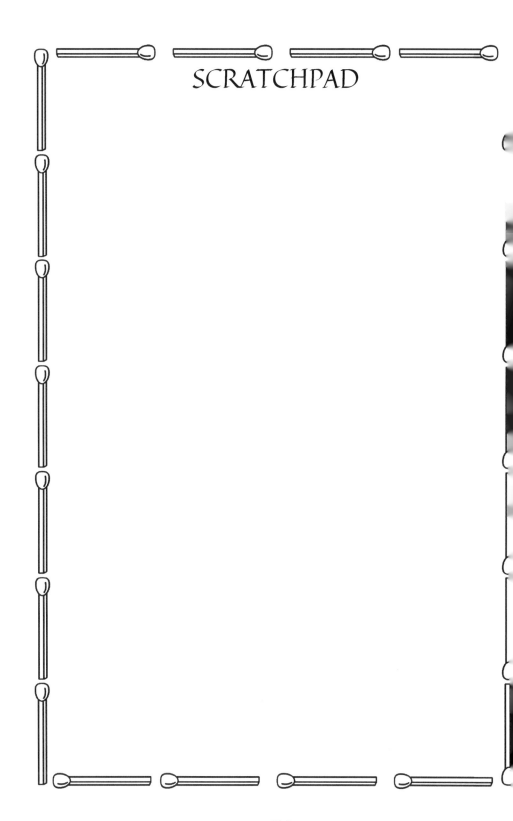

SCRATCHPAD

ANSWERS

1.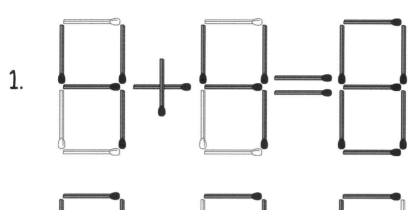

2.

3.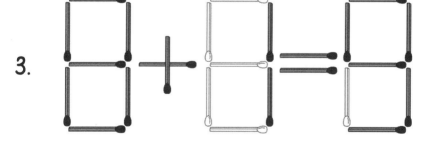

4.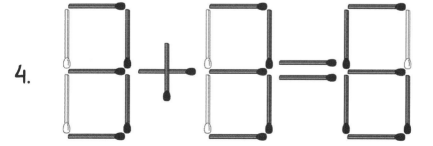

ANSWERS

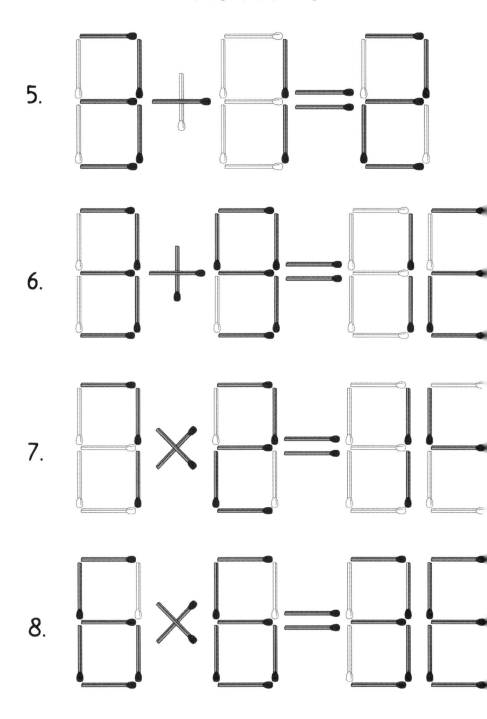

5.

6.

7.

8.

ANSWERS

9.

10.

11.

12.

ANSWERS

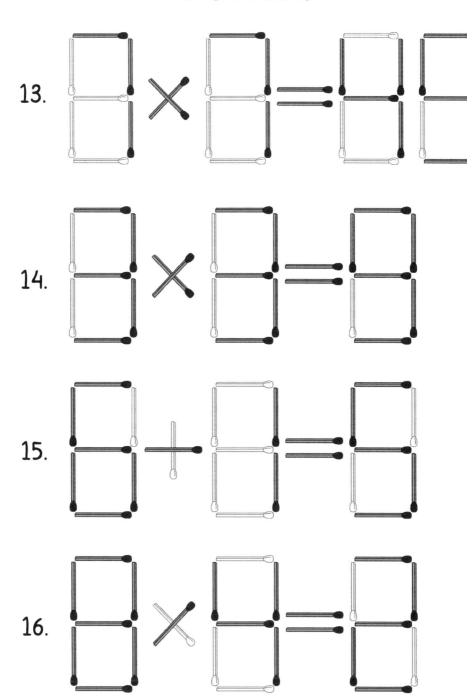

13.

14.

15.

16.

ANSWERS

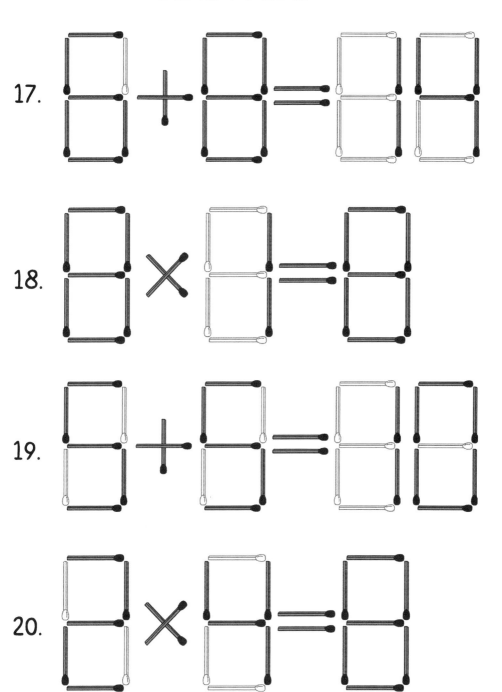

ANSWERS

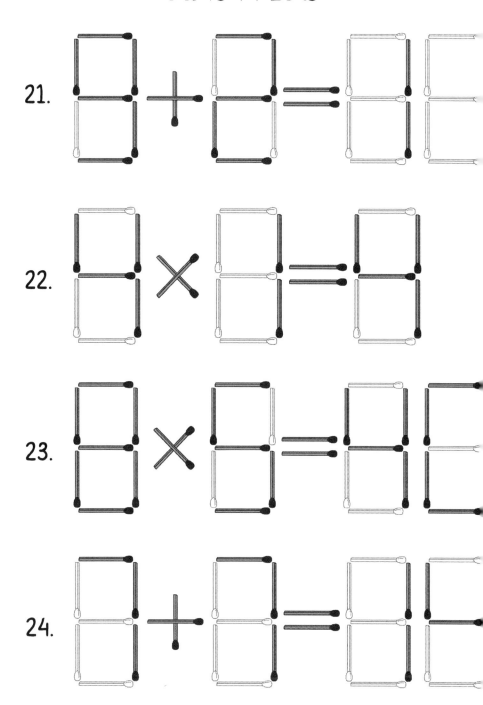

21.

22.

23.

24.

ANSWERS

25.

26.

27.

28.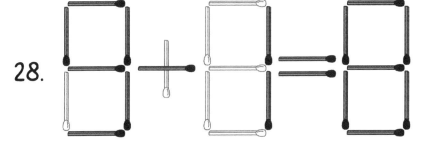

ANSWERS

29.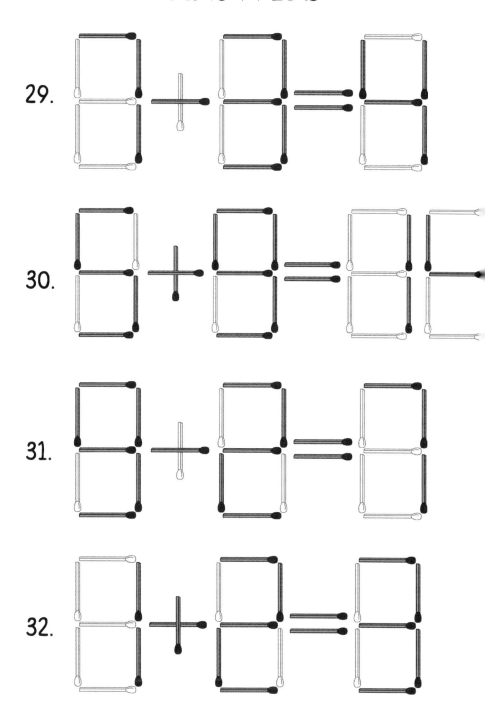

30.

31.

32.

ANSWERS

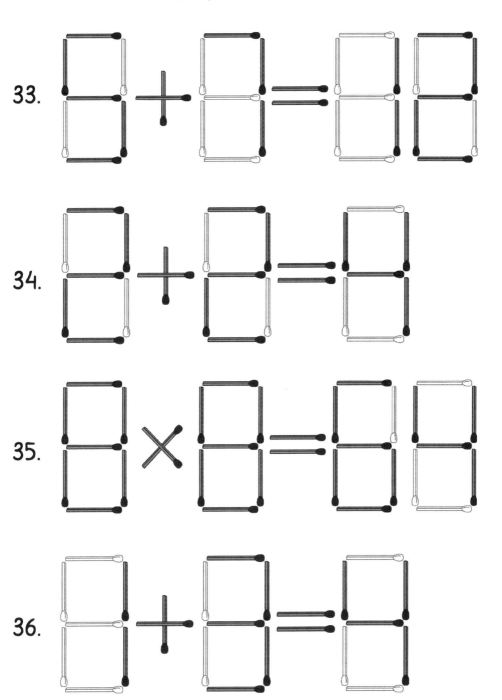

33.

34.

35.

36.

ANSWERS

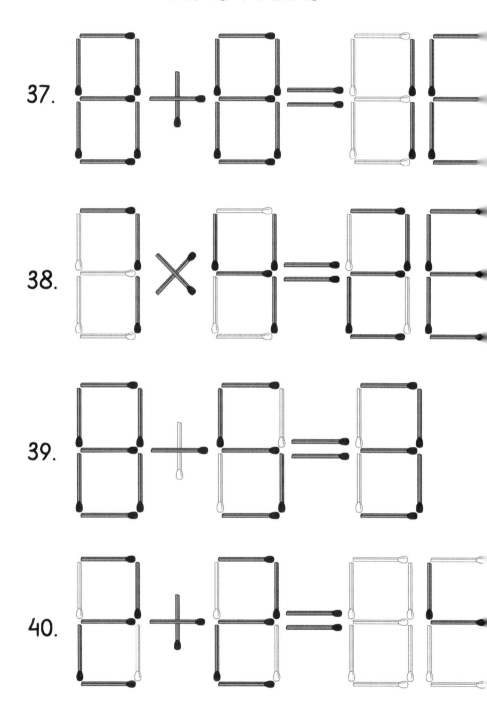

37.

38.

39.

40.

ANSWERS

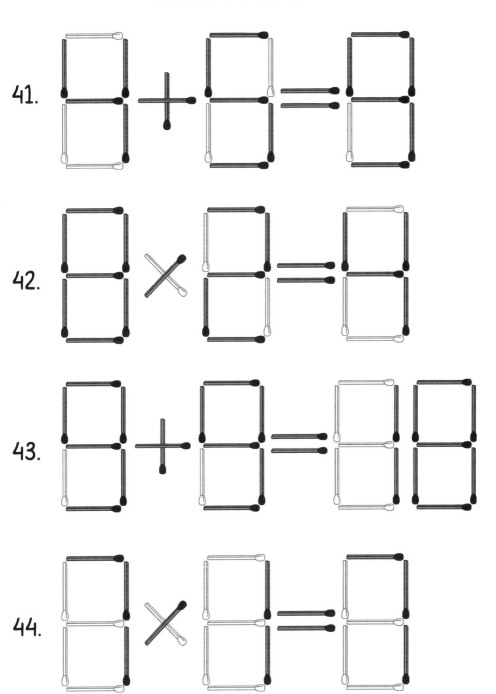

41.

42.

43.

44.

ANSWERS

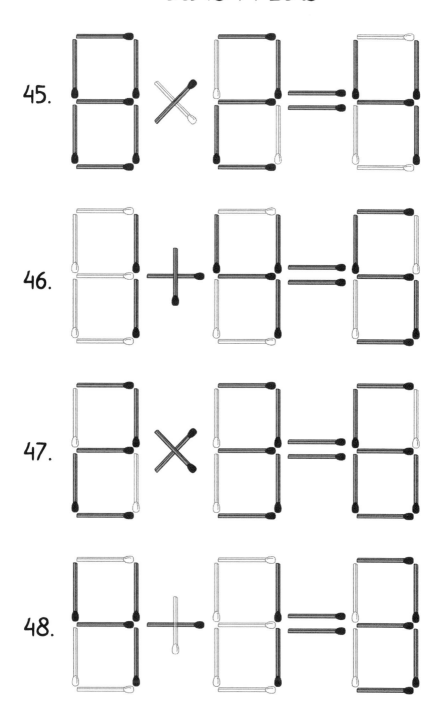

45.

46.

47.

48.

ANSWERS

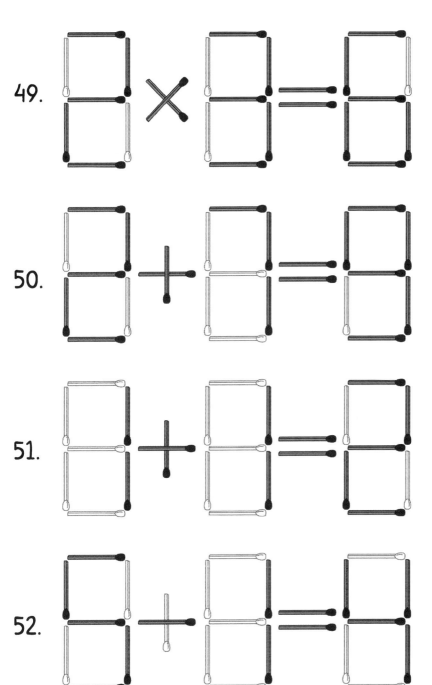

49.

50.

51.

52.

ANSWERS

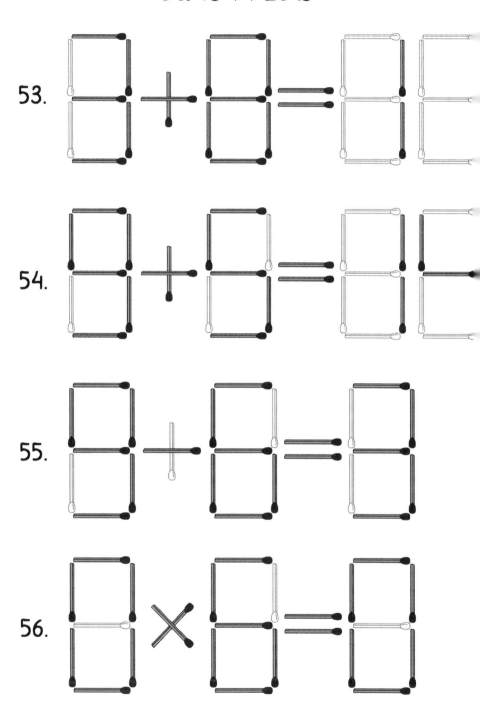

53.

54.

55.

56.

ANSWERS

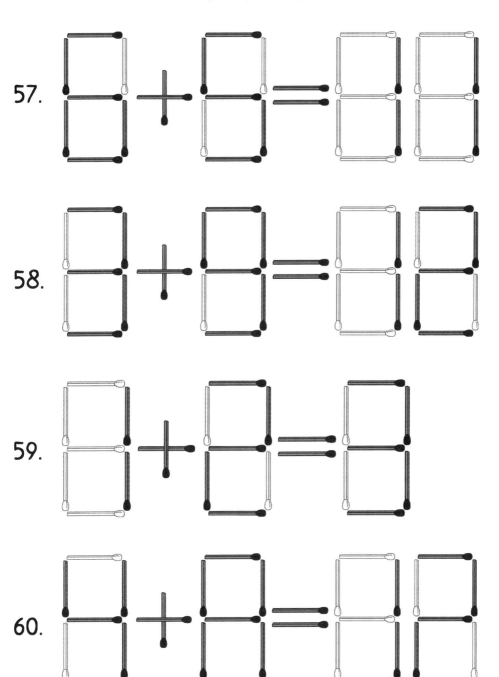

57.

58.

59.

60.

ANSWERS

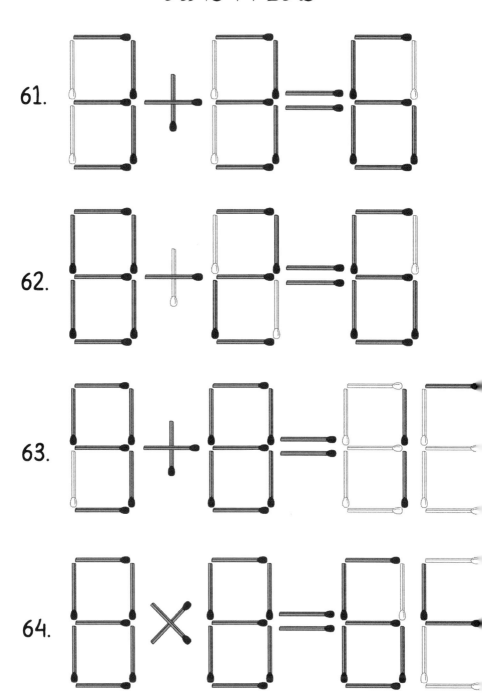

61.

62.

63.

64.

ANSWERS

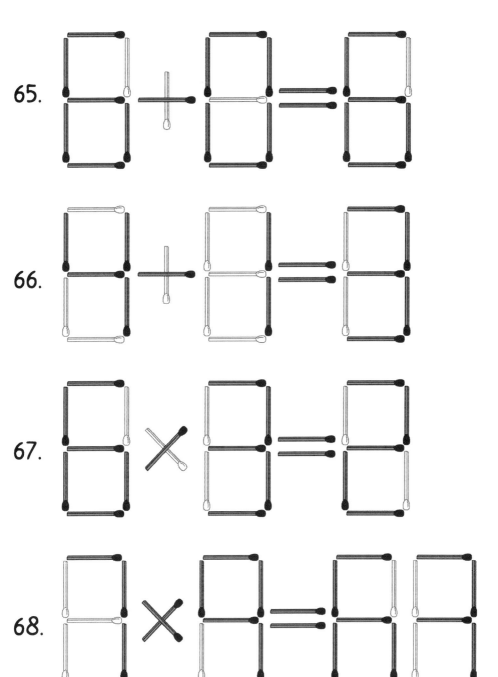

65.

66.

67.

68.

ANSWERS

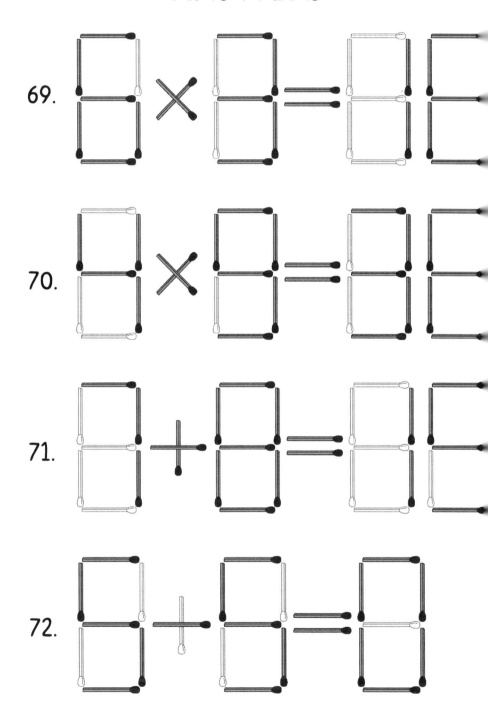

69.

70.

71.

72.

ANSWERS

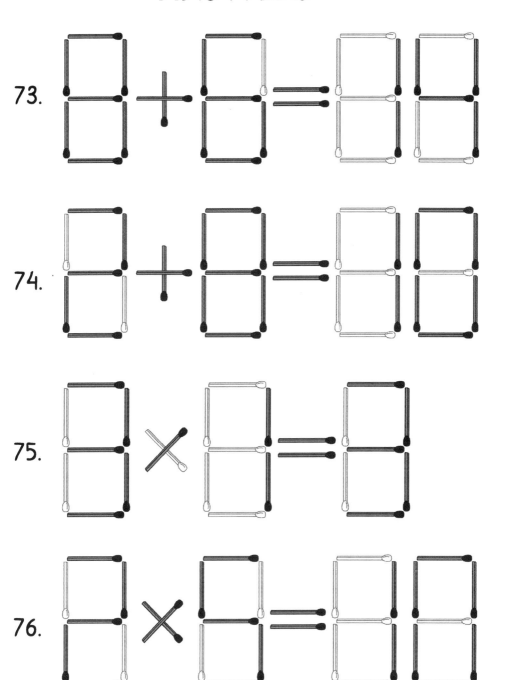

ANSWERS

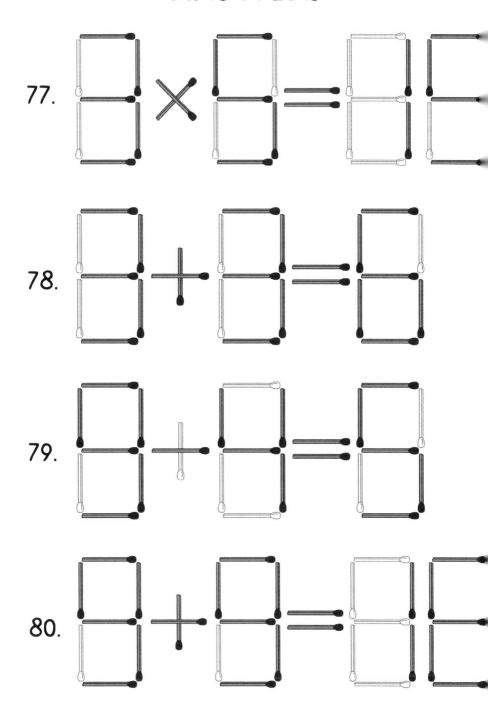

ANSWERS

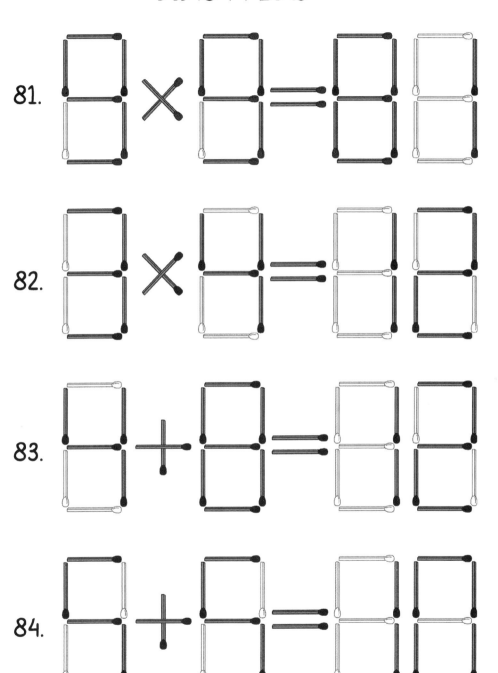

ANSWERS

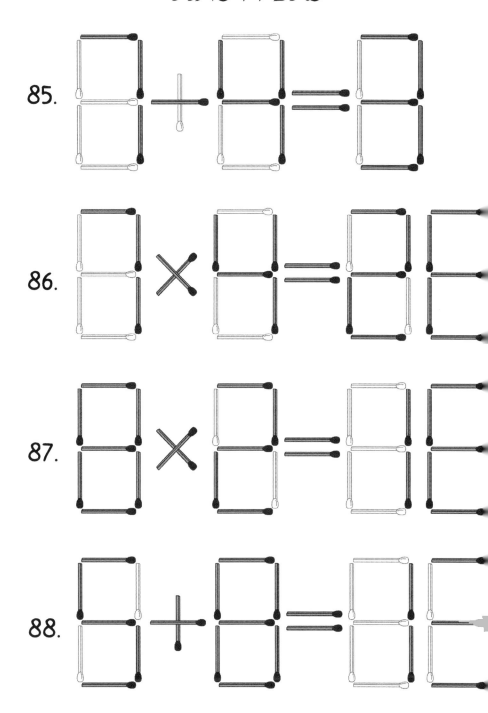

85.

86.

87.

88.

ANSWERS

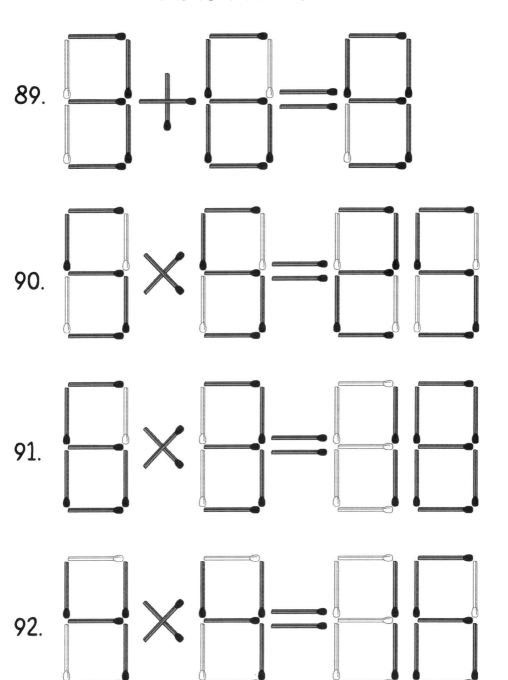

ANSWERS

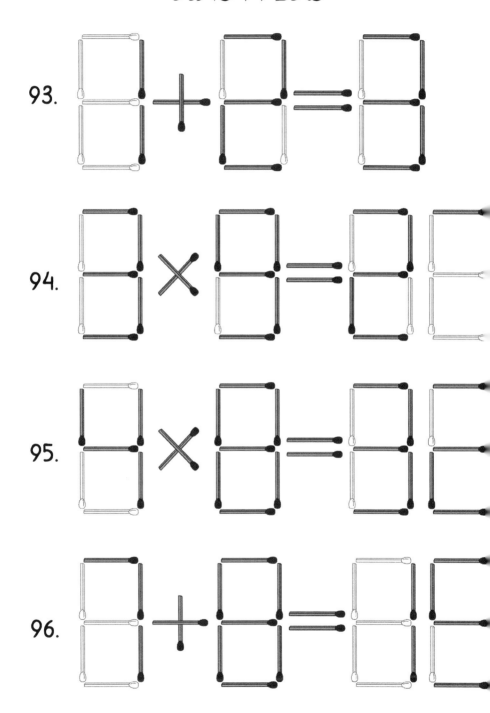

93.

94.

95.

96.

ANSWERS

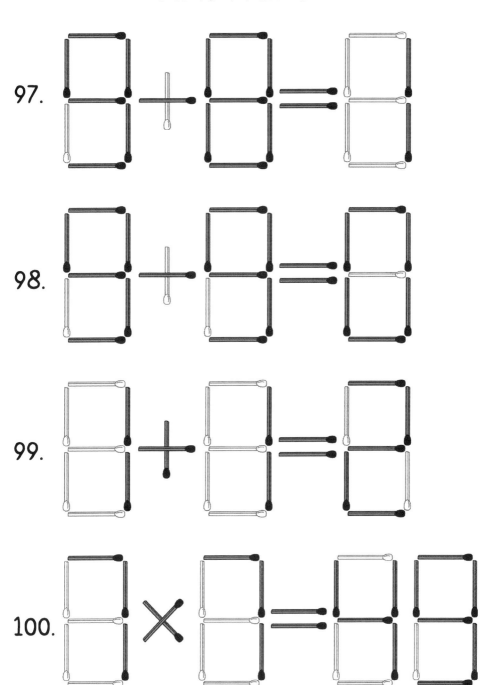

97.

98.

99.

100.

ANSWERS (BONUS)

1.

2.

3.

4.

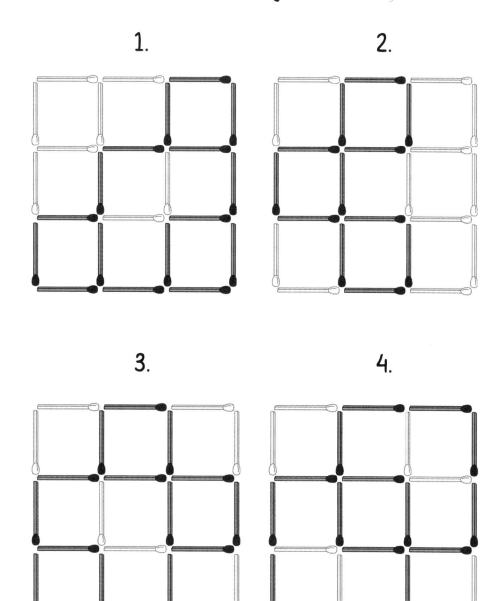

ANSWERS (BONUS)

5.

6.

7.

8.

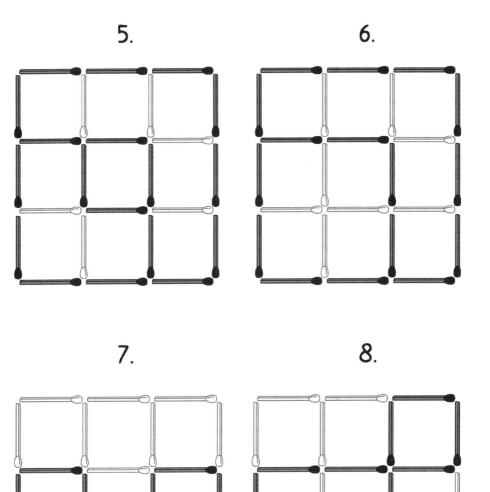

THE END

Please, if you liked the Matchstick Puzzles, leave me rating and a comment on the Amazon website.

Thank you :-)

Made in the USA
Las Vegas, NV
29 November 2024